GOD'S BATTLE AXE

OLOHIRERE EZOMO

GOD'S BATTLE AXE

OLOHIRERE EZOMO

Cover Design by Oluwatoyinbo Odediran
Inner Design by Aqua Media & Publishing

ISBN: 978-31064-2-2.

Published by AquaPub, an imprint of Aqua Media & Publishing

To my cherished friends and co-laborers in
Christ, who share my deep desire to become a
battle axe for the Kingdom's use.

And to missionaries reaching the unreached
with the richness of the gospel of Grace.

ACKNOWLEDGEMENTS

To God, my Chief cornerstone, my anchor and strength. Thank you for being much more than I could ever imagine to me. Thank you for lifting me from the miry clay of sin and causing me to seat among kings. ONLY YOUR GRACE COULD HAVE BROUGHT ME THIS FAR.

"I became a servant of the gospel by the gift of God' grace given me through the working of his power. Although I am less than the least of God's people, this grace was given me: to preach to the gentiles the unsearchable riches of Christ. Ephesians 3:7-8."

Pastor Tolu Mala, thank you for being a burning firebrand, lighting up the way for generations to come. May the anointing of God over your life never run dry. Great grace sir!

To my great friends, too numerous to list and precious family members, thank you for your support, encouragement and prayers. God bless you. *"Always remember that your labour in the Lord is not in vain."* *1Corinthians 15:58b.*

To every willing heart that will pick up this piece, read it and choose to begin a fresh experience with the Master, thank you for gladdening my heart!

CONTENT

FOREWORD

I feel greatly honoured to be asked to write this foreword to a maiden work by a budding Christian writer. I have known Olohi for 8 years and her passion for God, commitment to God and consecration to God has been unrivaled and unparalled. She indeed have a great hunger for God and missions which is the heart beat of God. Olohi is a rare gift to this generation and this piece in your hand is a reflection of the deposit of God upon her life.

God is indeed raising battle axes in this end time that will take the battle to the gates of the enemy in order to recover that which the devil has taken. This book is a challenge to every believer to rise up and be relevant, useful and active in the Kingdom at such a time as this. The character studies are so insightful, deep and full of great lessons that believers ought to emulate. Many believers who go to church in this dispensation, go with beggarly minds to get from God and so that their needs can be met. Many are also carried away by the prosperity theology that God can bless us and prosper us. It is sad to note that many believers are therefore ignorant of the fact that they are blessed already.

Ephesians 1:3, "Blessed be the God and Father of our Lord Jesus Christ, who hath blessed us with ALL spiritual blessings in Heavenly places in Christ"

Many are always after what they will get from God and not what they themselves will give to God. Only those who consecrate themselves will give to God's battle axe this end time will do great exploit.

I urge you as you read, to please have a change of mind and become a battle axe in the hands in the hands of God at this strategic time in the Kingdom.

God is looking for vessels.

Ezekiel 22:30, "And I sought for a man among them, that should make up the hedge and stand in the gap before me for the land, that I should not destroy it but I found none".

If it is not; then when?
If it is not you ; then who?
If it is not here ; then where?

I commend this book to all believers, students, youth, adults, ministers in God's vineyard who have chosen to be vessels in the hands of the Master, Jesus our Lord and Savior.

Great grace!

Simon Babs Mala
November 2013

THE MASTER'S DESIRE

THE MASTER'S DESIRE

Matthew 24;3-5

"As Jesus was sitting on the Mount of Olives, the disciples came to him privately, "Tell us, " they said, "when will this happen, and what will be the sign of your coming and of the end of the age? " Jesus answered, "Watch out that no one deceives you. For many will come in my name, claiming, "I am the Christ," and will deceive many".

Beloved , the second coming of the master is loser than we could ever imagine. I do not know the exact time or hour, but this one thing I know, it is closer than when we first believed. This explains why the battle has become fiercer than ever before. The kingdom of darkness is on the rampage, the devil has resorted to unimaginable and unprecedented methods to battle the children of God to standstill. Little wonder then, that the world seems to have infiltrated the church. Pollution and wanton sinfulness has become the order of the day. Simply put, the devil has gone crazy in his bid to win.

Unfortunately, he seems to have forgotten that his fate had been determined long ago, even before the foundations of the earth. He is fighting a lost battle. Yet, this does not give us liberty as believers to rest. Rather , it is a drive for us to fight courageously for the faith of our fathers.

The Master's desire therefore is to raise an end time army, fashioned and equipped as battle axes for the Master's use. Men and women that have answered the call to go wherever He sends them , do whatever He asks them to do and fight till their last breath is gone. If there is any time the world was ripe for Good news , it is NOW!

Men and women that would be in the world but not of the world . Men and women that would occupy the corridors of power in our schools, institutions, hospitals, politics, office, markets, etc., and bring about revivals that will draw souls to Him.

Our emphasis thus, as we go through the pages of the book together would be the need of the Master in this end time for available battleaxes, the implication and cost of being useful tool in the hands of the Master.

Are you a professional in a particular field, a student, a missionary? Journey with me through the pages of this piece as we unveil the core of the Master' desire for this time and see how we can plant ourselves right within his will. Such that, the things that matter to Jesus would matter to us, the things that grieve His heart would grieve our hearts and the thing that bring Him joy would be our priority.

Ezomo Olohirere
April, 2010

GOD'S BATTLE AXE

Listen to the master' pleadings,
There is urgent work for all,
Head the spirit's interceding,
Give this answer to the call.

Many souls in sin are dying,
Haste to help them while you may,
For the time is swiftly flying,
Will you now to Jesus say?

I am ready for service for thee, dear Lord,
I am willing to be what you'd have me be,
I will go to where you want me to go,
I am ready for service for thee, dear Lord.

Here am I, send me,
Tho' the pathway seems dark,
For thee I'll do or die
I am ready for service Lord.

Joseph Lincoln Hall 1866-1930

WHO IS A
BATTLE AXE?

1 WHO IS A BATTLE AXE?

Jeremiah 51:20-21

"You are my war club, my weapon for battle. With you I shatter nations, with you I destroy kingdoms, with you I shatter horse and rider, with you I shatter chariot and driver"

WHAT IS A BATTLE AXE?

Webster's dictionary defines a battle axe with a wide blade, used as a weapon of war, more common in ancient times. It is an axe specifically designed for combat. They are specialized versions of the common axes used domestically. Besides axes designed for combat, there are many axes that could be used as tools and weapons. Some could even be used as projectiles especially the lighter ones. It is usually with a blade made of wrought iron or carbon steel, the battle axe is very sharp in order to inflict grievous wounds to the offender.

Contextually, the above verses were taken from a chapter that occurred in a setting of a "bounce book". Israel and Judah had committed grievous sins against Go. They had allowed themselves to be drawn into trap of idolatry that was rampant those days. Rather than repent, they only became worse. They fell prey to the worship of other gods that God specifically warned them against. Yet, God in His infinite mercy, sent messengers and prophets to remind them of the covenant they had with him.

Jeremiah 51:5b *"For Israel and Judah have not been forsaken by their God, the Lord Almighty, though THEIR LAND IS FILLED WITH GUILT BEFORE THE HOLY ONE OF ISRAEL".*

They had forgotten their first love. Israel had forgotten her rock! God, out of anger decided to chastise them in love. Mankind has a way of retracing his steps when hit with the storm of affliction. This brought about the choice of Babylon as a judgment wand. A nation that would take Israel into captivity and then peradventure, they will remember again to call on the God of their salvation. Babylon was that battle axe, that weapon of war to inflict injury on the Israelites. Please note, not because He had given up on them but because He was giving them an opportunity to repent and come back. God later punished Babylon for her pride and restored Israel when she repented.

God in His love will not forsake us forever. Though He slays us in anger for our sins yet he is easily entreated when we seek His face. That is why the scriptures records in 2Chronicles 7:14

"If my people, who are called by my name, will humble themselves and pry, and seek my face, and turn from their wicked ways; then will I hear from heaven, and will forgive their sin, and will heal their land".

Such is the loving kindness of the God we serve, even when we are unfaithful, He always remains faithful. Beloved, God always has a need per time. And He is always on the lookout for men that can be used to carry out his purpose. If He could use a wicked nation like Babylon, how much more will He be willing to use His children for His good pleasures.

ROLES OF A BATTLE AXE

WHEN God refers to a man or woman as a battle axe, there are roles or purposes such a person will subserve.
1. To break nations in pieces and to destroy the kingdom of darkness.
2. To take the battle to the gate of the enemy
3. To declare and ensure the will of God
4. To possess the land for Christ
5. To drive revival on the land

1. *To break the nations in pieces and to destroy the kingdom of darkness.*

One of the characteristics of the battle axe is that it is used to inflict grievous wounds on the offender. One of the desires of God is that mankind will crush the head of the enemy ultimately despite attacks on our heels.

Genesis 3:15, " And I will put enmity between you and the woman, and between your offspring's and hers. He (mankind) will crush your head, and you (serpent) will strike his heel".

One of the reasons why God has placed us as believers on earth is to shine as light thereby destroying the works of darkness. Jesus is the light of the world and because we carry Him in us, we spread the light wherever we go. Wherever light dominates, darkness cannot survive there. Believers as light of the world are to:

- To separate good from evil
- For signs and wonders
- Give direction and a sense of purpose
- Understand the times and what to be done.

A battle axe for Christ is to populate the Kingdom of Christ. A battle axe is someone who has determined to live and devote the total sum of his energy, by virtue of position or any acquisition, to bring souls to the

Kingdom. Soldiers, whose singular mission is to destroy anything that represents the kingdom of darkness via fervent intercessory prayers, daring missionary outreaches or by means within their disposal.

2. *Will take the battle to the gate of the enemy.*
Most Christians nowadays are very cowardly. Many times we do not seem to understand the faith we have embraced. Many are ready to compromise even at the slightest provocation. We forget that we belong to the Lion of the tribe of Judah . Many believers dread the devil. Many of our prayer point can attest to this. Little wonder why our prayers seem not to be answered because most are borne out of fear and not faith. Many do not understand the privilege position they occupy in Christ .some on the other hand are just complacent, not willing to in a way 'disturb' the devil so that he does not attack them in anger. To survive in these last days, beloved, you must be courageous.

2Chronicles 15:8, *"When Asa heard these words and the prophecy of Azariah son of Oded the prophet, he took courage. He removed the detestable idols from the whole land of Judah and Benjamin and from the towns he had captured in the hills of Ephraim . he repaired the alter of the Lord that was in front of the portico of the Lord's temple".*

Just like King Asa took courage and established the

standard of God in his land, a battle axe also is someone who does not run in fear of the devil. A battle axe is someone who by reason of study and maturity has come to understand his/her position in Christ and so can stand boldly to contend for the faith of our fathers. Not only that, but will also take the battle to the gate of the enemy.

A battle axe is indeed a son who understands and fulfills the words of Apostle John in 1 John 2:14 that "I write to you young men because you are strong and the word of God lives in you and you have overcome the evil one" and "You, der children, are from God and have overcome them, because the One who is in you is greater than the one who is in the world" (1John 4:4).

3. *Will declare and ensure the will of God.*
A battle axe is a pillar. A pillar is a vital structure in any architectural building. It provides strength and support for the structure. Without it, any building will collapse at the slightest wind.

By comparison then, a battle axe will stand solidly for God anytime and anywhere. Standing for righteousness and holiness is his/her hallmark. Please note, I am not referring to the self righteous and pious attitude some people exhibit in a bid to show themselves better than others. No! Not at all. I am referring to that meek and gentle spirit that Jesus displayed while on His earthly sojourn.

I tell people that you do not need to announce to us that you are born again. By your fruits, we will know. Matthew 7: 16a, *"By their fruits you will recognize them…"* Therefore a battle axe is someone who can exert Godly influence and impact wherever they find themselves. It is heartbreaking to see a lot of firebrand and tongue speaking Christians, who during their campus days carried fire and zeal for the things of God , mess up during their youth service days because the people that used to know them as brother or sister are no longer around.

Beloved, a battle axe cannot be a spiritual baby, tossed to and fro by every wind of doctrine. A battle axe knows the mind of God from scriptures and has a deep personal relationship with God. Not just that, He also stands to declare His will and ensure it through personal obedience. Matthew 6:10, *"Your Kingdom come, your will be done on earth as it is in heaven"*.

The will of God has been established in heaven because that is God's habitation but here on earth, for the will and purpose of God to be established anywhere and in any situation, we must pray it to be. He establishes His will mainly through people willing to obey Him. A battle axe, therefore, will offer himself or herself as a doer of God's will, asking Him to guide, lead and give the means to accomplish His purposes.

4. *Possess the land*

To possess means "to have ownership of ", 'to enter into" or "control". Right from creation, God's desire was for mankind to have control and subdue His other works of creation.

Genesis 2:28, *"God blessed them and said to them, Be fruitful and increase in number, fill the earth and subdue it. Rule over the fish of the sea and the birds of the air and over every living creature that moves on the ground."*

The sole purpose of this was for the glory of God to be reveled in all of creation. The psalmist in his appreciation of man as the Lord's creation said: *"… You made him ruler over the works of your hands; you put everything under his feet"* Psalms 8:6.

When Jesus had finished his earthly sojourn, He gave an instruction to His disciples to occupy the earth till His second return. To occupy means "to invest" or "to do business with".

Luke 19:13, *"So he called ten of his servants and gave them ten minas. "Put this money to work," he said, 'UNTIL I COME BACK."*.

A battle axe for God is a profitable servant. A servant that will use all his talents for the advancement of the Kingdom.

Beloved , we must possess our workplaces, our schools, our churches etc. we must pray that the will of God be done and take over for Jesus radically. It is still the Lord's desire that man, especially believers, would possess the land for Him. That is one of the assignments of a battle axe.

Obadiah 1:17, *"But on Mount Zion will be deliverance; it will b holy, and the house of Jacob will possess its inheritance."*

5.   *To drive revival on the land.*
Psalms 44:1, *"We have heard with our ears, O God ; our fathers told us what you did in their days, in days long ago."*

Many years ago, during a retreat, while lifting up my voice to God, crying that he sends the fire of revival into the church again, I heard the quiet whisper of the Holy Spirit asking where the vessels He is to pour the fire on were? He went on to explain that if He pours out anointing on the bare ground (in the absence of vessels) there would only b erosion. The truth is that we need this reawakening like never before. Revival means freshness. It ushers in great manifestations of the power of God and the readiness of people to submit to God.

(Psalms 110:3). Righteousness and holiness are prerequisites for such visitation. Times of revival are marked by intense spiritual growth, genuine Christian conversations, excellent family life, government stability and economic bloom.

Yet for us to experience such refreshing times there must be ready vessels, willing to be forerunners of such dispensations. Men and women that will allow the Holy spirit to fill them and work through them to challenge sin and proclaim The Good News. Such drivers of revival like Apostles Paul and Peter reported to have turned the world upside down, Daniel who brought about the deliverance and revival of his people after the stipulated 70 years of captivity, Moses who through the mighty hand of God led the children of Israel from bondage enroute the Promised Land, Smith Wigglesworth who ushered in the Pentecostal radical faith in the healing ministry, David Livingstone who brought the Good news to Africa, Kathryn Kuhlman that ushered in a dispensation of sweet fellowship with the Holy Spirit and great healings, Apostle Joseph Ayo Babalola and Pa S.G. Elton of blessed memory, who pioneered the Pentecostal revival in Nigeria. Such is the description of God's battle axe; drivers or forerunners of the end time revival.

REAPERS ARE NEEDED

Hark, to the music resounding,
Reapers are needed today;
Fields are all white, to the harvest
Let us be up and away!
Ever the Master is calling,
Hasten! The shadows are falling;
On the harvest field,
Gather the golden yield,
Precious sheaves.

Forward with hearts full of gladness,
Reapers, I pray you, make haste;
Grain there is ready and waiting;
If not soon gathered, will waste;
Then let us hear you replying,
Labor with undying courage,
Send up a word of cheer,
Tell of the rest so near,
Rest at home.

Lizzie DeArmond

Chapter Two

WHY THIS NEED?

2 WHY THIS NEED?

Romans 8:19 and 22

"The creation waits in eager expectation for the sons of God to be revealed… We know that the whole creation has been groaning as in the pains of childbirth right up to the present time".

There has never been a time when God needs vessels He can equip as His battle axes as much as now. The spirit of God has spoken expressly through prophecies and visions that God is raising an end time army. If you are sensitive enough, you will also realize that the stage is being set for the emergence of new leaders in our churches and in fact, all spheres of life. For a church and I see our fathers in the faith, great patriarchs that have done excellently and fought valiantly for the cause of the Kingdom. But inevitably, many of them are already having gray hairs and their physical strength dwindling even though they still carry the visions God gave them alive and growing. My burden thus, is who will be the next Pastor E.A. Adeboye, the next Pastor W.F. Kumuyi, the next Reverend Mike Oye, the next Brother Gbile Akanni and the likes? I cannot but ask where the next generation of God' Generals are.

Where are the likes of Smith Wigglesworth that will heal people through radically generated faith? Where are the likes of Kathryn Kuhlman that would bask in the palpable power of the Holy Ghost to deliver and work the mystery of salvation? Where are the great evangelists of our time that will plead earnestly with heaven to open ancient gates of nations or they die s John Knox did with Scotland? Where are the missionaries of our time who will risk everything the world cherishes just to take light to them that still seat in darkness? Where are they?

Oh! If only we will be sensitive enough to hear the cry of our Father, looking and searching for men, vessels who will be ready to be sent. The harvest is truly plenteous but the laborers are few.

Matthew 9:37, *"Then He said to the disciples, "The harvest is plentiful but the workers are few. Ask the Lord of the harvest, therefore, to send out workers into His harvest field'.*

God seeks for men earnestly because we do not have much time left. He needs vessels to transform their niche for God. Are you a professor? The four walls of your university is your niche, your students especially those assigned to you must be impacted. Are you a student? Your class is your niche; your room is your niche, . Your roommate should feel the awesome presence of God radiating from your life. Are you medical personnel? Your ward, your patients are your mission fields. Win as many as possible with your kind words and diligent service. Beloved, mankind is at a critical phase where he needs the divinity of God to step into his affairs. A time when the presence of God is the only panacea of the aching vacuum in the hearts of men.

Ultimately, we should employ every means possible, in the shortest time possible, to preach the simplicity of The Good News either in words, actions or both.

… the battle line had been drawn

Revelations 12:7-11
"And there was war in Heaven, Michael and his angels fought against the dragon, and the dragon and his angels fought back. But he was not strong enough and they lost their place in heaven. The great dragon was hurled down —that ancient serpent called the devil, or Satan who leads the whole world astray. He was hurled to the earth and his angels with him. Then I heard a loud voice in heaven say: Now have come salvation an the power and

the kingdom of our God, and the authority of His Christ. For the accuser of our brothers, who accuses them before our God day and night, has been hurled down. They overcame him by the blood of the lamb and by the word of their testimony: they did not love their lives so much as to shrink from death".

Imagine two different families – A and B contending tenaciously for a piece of land. After months of grueling tossing of law suits (with possible use of charms against each other), the court finally judges in favor of family A. Family A walks away basking in her victory but watching her back cautiously for any fight back from family B, family B goes off angrily looking for any means possible to revenge. They become sworn enemies. Children born into both families are told the ancient tory and enmity is transferred from generation to generation.

The same way, the battle line between believers and the devil had been drawn after that fight that devil lost in Heaven. The serpent will always look for ways always look for ways to bruise the heel of man and man will crush his head. You see, in the spiritual world, you are either for or against God . You cannot be in between . You cannot stand on the fence. There are two sides to this battle; God and Satan, light and darkness, good and evil, truth and falsehood. The day you got saved, you were translated from the kingdom of darkness to the

Kingdom of light; you shifted from the side of evil to good, from Satan's camp to God's camp. If you belong to Jesus, your life is now hid in Christ. *Colossians 3:3, "For you died, and your life is now hidden with Christ in God".*

… and the war is ongoing

Revelations 12: 17
"Then the dragon was enraged at the woman and went off to make war against the rest of her offspring - those who obey God's commandments and hold to the testimony of Jesus."

Apostle Paul, in Ephesians 6:10, affirm that we are in a continuous spiritual battle as believers. Amazingly though, the scriptures reminds us again and again that our weapons of warfare are not canal but mighty through God. This is because the battle we are fighting is not physical nut spiritual. So also, as a battle axe, you are a spiritual battle axe.

The war is still being staged but the outcome has been determined. The crucial blow came to satan when the lamb, Jesus Christ shed His blood for our sins and resurrected on the third day. He conquered death, grave and satan. Stan and his followers have been defeated and will ultimately be destroyed in the lake that burns with brimstone at the second coming of our Lord. Nevertheless, satan is battling daily to bring more into his ranks and to keep his own from deflecting to God's side.

As believers, Christ has assured us of victory. God will not lose and in fact, cannot lose the battle. But we must ensure that we do not lose the battle over our souls. Beloved, a great spiritual battle is being fought. The devil will do anything and everything to win but the same way he was not strong enough in the initial battle in Heaven, so he still is. Therefore, we must take up our positions as soldiers, ever ready, because there is no time for indecision.

….yet the time is short

Revelations 12:12
"Therefore rejoice you heavens and you who dwell in them! But woe to the earth and the sea, because the devil has gone down to you! He is filled with fury, BECAUSE HE KNOWS THAT HIS TIME IS SHORT!

Desperately and intensely, the devil is fighting. When we look around the world, we see so much depravity that makes you shudder. Sometimes, I wonder how wicked the heart of man is. Acts that were considered alien have now become the order of the day. Incidences of rape, incest, gay marriages (even among priests), suicide bombing, gruesome murders have filled our newspaper pages. It seems our world is going crazy. Beloved there are just signs that the devil is exploring every means possible to draw men to his side. Unfortunately, I must say, that many Christians are being distracted by pressures and disappointments. Alarmingly I have begun to ask the same question Jesus asked in Luke 18:8b, *"However, when the Son of Man comes, will He find faith on the earth?"* Will He still find men holding the fort? Will He still find you and me watching?

The devil understands that his time is short but do you understand that your time is short too? Are you sure you are not buying and selling while forgetting the primary purpose and goals? Hope you have not forgotten that we are strangers and pilgrims here on earth? I remember a patient of mine that was suffering from a terminal illness and I wanted to minister the prayer of deliverance to her. Unfortunately , she died in the early hours of the morning before I could reach her. Oh, how I wept for God's forgiveness. I wished I had done it earlier. Stop procrastinating! You do not have all the time. Tomorrow might be too late! Is there someone God has placed a burden in your heart to minister to? Is there an assignment God has given you to do? Is there a soul you must win? Do so now. Please, do not wait till you finish your course; do not wait till the atmosphere is perfect because it may never be. Do not wait till you get married, get the car or build that house, DO IT NOW!

CHARACTER STUDY:
EZRA
RUTH

3 CHARACTER STUDY: **EZRA** **RUTH**

One day, as I sat down in my study, going through the pages of the Bible , I realized that God used various people , at various times and in diverse circumstances to carry out His own divine task and plans. What struck me in awesome wonder was the simplicity of the background of a lot of these people. There was hardly any sentiment for any particular race or tribe, profession or gender; they were mostly people that were usually not reckoned with in the so called important matters. They were not necessarily the most educated, neither were they the wealthiest. They were not the oldest or the wisest. They were simply simple! They were usually the neglected citizens, the crude professionals, the weakest , the shy, the introverts, the dropouts and the downtrodden. They were just ordinary men and women who used by an extra ordinary God to carry out supernatural exploits.

These were people who had life changing encounters with Jesus. They tapped into the grace of God and that changed the story of their lives for good. How else shall we explain the salvation of the whole generation of Jews by an orphan girl Esther, or the inclusion in the lineage of grace of that prostitute Rahab or the conversation of Paul – a world acclaimed church terrorist to a world celebrated gospel crusader? It was grace. Nothing but what amazing grace that saves a wretch, that saved you and I, that embraced us even in our sins and gave us a right standing with our maker.

As we look into the lives of some of our biblical heroes and see lessons we may glean from their walk with God, we must do this on the anchor of our understanding of the role that the amazing grace of God played in each of their lives. This grace is divine, that is, it comes from God; and it is a gift to mankind. It is that divine influence that inspires our hearts to embrace the gift of salvation, spurs us on to ill and desire virtuous things. It regenerates and sanctifies. It imparts strength to do the seemingly impossible , to endure trials and resist temptations.

1Corinthians 15:9-10, "For I am the least of the apostles and do not even deserve to be called an apostle, because I persecuted the church of God. BUT BY THE GRACE OF GOD, I am what I am, and his grace to me was not without effect. No, I worked harder than all of them – yet not I , but the grace of God that was with me".

Grace is basically the empowering presence of God that enables and strengthen us to be all He created us to be and to effectively carry out all He asks us to do. As I write this section, the song amazing grace begins to play in my mind, reminding me again of the deep words of this beautiful hymn. This grace manifests in diverse ways: saves a wretch, restores sight to the blind, brings the lost back home to the loving embrace of the father teaches our heart to fear God, sheds the love of Christ abroad in our hearts and helps to love even the unlovable, keeps us pure and spotless, leading us through our pilgrim journey to our final home!. O, how my heart is greatly humbled and my eyes filled with tears when I imagine what my life would have been without this grace. Beloved, if you are reading this piece and you have not sincerely experienced this grace or you are continually frustrating the grace of God over your life by living in sin, would you stop now and ask the Holy Spirit to forgive you. Will you confess your sins to God and ask the Holy Spirit to fill your heart with strength and power to resist sin. Thereafter, please determine to live for Jesus every hour, every day.

Our first character study is Ezra.

EZRA

Different people have people they celebrate for different reasons. When asked to list celebrities, names like Ben Carson for those intrigued by medicine may come first, while football fans would list their favorite football stars. They are usually remembered because of something good and great they have done. Also in biblical settings, great men abound. But, far from being well known, this unheralded man of God named Ezra deserves recognition. Ezra, a man of God and a true hero, was a model for Israel and is a fitting model for us.

The first mention of Ezra in the scriptures was in 1 Chronicles 4:17 when the genealogy of the tribes of Israel were being mentioned. From there, we see that Ezra was mentioned as belonging to the tribe of Judah. Ezra 7:1 – 5 goes further by helping us trace his lineage better. Notably, he was the son of Seraiah and descendent of Aaron the Chief Priest. So, his full name may most likely have been Priest Ezra Seraiah. There is no mention of his wife but we know that had children, specifically: Jether, Mered, Epher and Jalon. Little is known about his upbringing as the records we have focus on the part of his life spent in Babylon and Jerusalem. However, careful study of his life reveals that:

- His life counted for God
- He was a man of the word
- He obeyed the instructions of God
- He was a teacher of the word
- He set a standard of repentance

1. *Our first lesson: Until your life begins to counts for God, Heaven may continue flipping the pages of your life as blank pages.* Unfortunately, several Christians go through life living for themselves. When the master opens your record in heaven, will He find notable acts of stewardship recorded against your name? if He asks you what you have done with the gifts, talents and opportunities He gave you. What will be your response? If each day you spend represents a page in the book that bears record of your life, would there be anything significant for heaven to document? Let your life begin to count!

About 80 years after rebuilding the temple under Zerubbabel, Ezra returned to Judah with about 2000 men and their families. But long before Ezra's mission began, he had allowed God to shape him.

Ezra 7:10, "For Ezra had devoted himself to the study and observance of the law of the Lord, and to teaching its decrees and laws in Israel".

2. Our second lesson: Ezra was a man of the word.

Any man that would be used by God as a battle axe, a vessel unto honour in His hand must be versed in the word of God. That is the soldier's major weapon for offense: the sword of the spirit (Ephesians 6:17). It starts first from an earnest desire to know more about God. To develop our relationship with the Holy Spirit, desiring the sincere milk of the word that we may grow thereby (1 Peter 2:2, Psalms 42:1).

Hosea 6:3. *"Let u acknowledge the lord. Let us press on to acknowledge Him. As surely as the sun rises He will appear; He will come to us like the winter rains, like the spring rains that water the earth."*

Ezra devoted himself to study of the word , how many believers can do that? In this age, the devil has done everything to distract us from the place of studying and meditating on the word with worldly pursuits and sometimes sadly enough, even our so called busy activities for God. We are often apt to jump out to do exploits for God , forgetting that the secret of our indomitable strength lies in the depth of the knowledge of God's word that we understand. The strength of every battle axe of God in this end time is the amount of the knowledge of God you possess. That was why Jesus taught His disciples to first be with Him before He sent them out to win souls. Mark 3:14 *"He appointed twelve — designating them apostles- that they might be with him and that he might send them out to preach,* " I am not talking about a shabby, shallow glimpse of what is written in the scriptures but rather , an in-depth, well-grounded understanding of God's will. Matthew 4:4 *"Jesus answered, "It is written. Man does not live on bread alone, but on every word that comes from the mouth of God".*

Ephesians 3:17-19, *"So that Christ may dwell in your hearts through faith. And I pray that you, being rooted and established in love, may have power together with all the saints, to grasp how wide and long and high and deep is the love of Christ, and to know this love that surpasses knowledge — that you may be filled to the measure of all fullness of God."*

3. *Our third lesson: Ezra obeyed to the instructions of God.*
To obey means to listen, to pay attention to something or someone. Many believers have heard the word so much, on Sundays, in bible studies, on radio etc. yet the word seems to be producing little or no fruit. The abundance of churches and several religious affiliations seems to have had little impact on our level of holiness. Beloved, may I ask you how many times you obey and follow what the word of God says. We are quick to quote it but slow to follow. The purpose of reading and studying the word of God is that we see our lives in the light of God's will and make the necessary amends to our lives. Only then can the word of God be said to be

fruitful in our lives. Remember when Jesus was interpreting the parable of the sower.

Matthew 13:19-22, *"When anyone hears the message about the kingdom and does not understand it, the evil one comes and snatches away what was sown in his heart. This is the seed sown along the path. The one who received the seed that fell on rocky places is the man who hears the word and at once receives it with joy. But since it has no root, he lasts only for a short time. When trouble or persecution comes because of the word, he quickly falls away. The one who received the seed that fell among thorns is the man who hears the word, but the worries of this life and the deceitfulness of wealth, choke it, making it unfruitful. But the one who received the seed that fell on good soil is the man who hears the word and understands it. HE PRODUCES A CROP, YIELDING A HUNDRED, SIXTY OR THIRTY TIMES WHAT WAS SOWN.*

Also, many struggle with the will of God for their lives. And even when they obey, it is partial. Beloved, God is not a half- measure God. It is either you obey 100% or not. 99.999% is not acceptable . 1 Samuel 15:22b; *"to obey is better than sacrifice, and to heed is better than the fat of rams"*.

4. *Our fourth lesson: Ezra knew the word so well that he was able to teach it.* A battle axe leads by example. A battle axe must live his/her life as a light set upon a hill, as an

epistle written for the world to read. Many teach people to do as they say but Jesus on several occasions taught his disciples by giving them a template based on the things he did or said, Acts 1:1, Luke 11:1.

Thus, when Ezra arrived in Judah and learned of the intermarriage between God's people and their pagan neighbors, he knew, based on his understanding from the unequal yoke. Rather than continue with the status quo, in obedience to standard of God's word, he rose up and taught the people the mandate of God. He wept, prayed and led the people to repentance. This later led to a national revival, Ezra chapters 9 and 10.

5. *Our fifth lesson: He set the standard of repentance by his own behavior.*

Ezra 10:1; *"While Ezra was praying and confessing, weeping and throwing himself down before the house of God, a large crowd of Israelites — men ,women and children- gathered around him. They too wept bitterly"*.

His weeping brought others to the point of sorrow. Some people may respond better when we tell them what to do and participate ourselves. When God places you in places of people within our sphere of interaction for good. The people knew God's word but were not motivated to do anything but when they saw Ezra, a well-respected leader, standing out and grieving, they realizing the enormity of their sins and returned.

Beloved , peradventure, God is raising you as the next Ezra for Nigeria or whatever nation you belong to, strategically locating you in a well-respected position to have first-hand exposure to the extent of corruption going on in the corridors of power. Would you stand and weep, pointing out the way of repentance, to bring about a wave of transparency and true service to the masses? Please, let God take you through His crucible of training, you cannot afford to fail God. Always remember Ezra, humble and obedient. Commit yourself to serving God as he did, with your whole life.

Let us also take a look at Sister Ruth Elimelech, the Moabites.

RUTH

Ruth 2:10-12

"At this she bowed with her face to the ground. She exclaimed, "Why have I found such favour in your eyes that you notice me — a foreigner?" Boaz replied, 'I have been told all about what you have done for your mother- in — law since the death of your husband — how you left your father and mother and your homeland and came to live a people you did not know before. May the Lord repay you for what you have done. May you be richly

rewarded by the Lord, the God of Israel, under whose wings you have come to take refuge"

Little is known about her childhood and lineage for reasons not known. But perhaps, they were not significant enough to earn a place in the Bible. Ruth was a young lady who fell in love with a foreigner from Judah. Year after year, she had struggled with the pain of childlessness. Probably , she tried appeasing the idols and gods of the land of Moab but all to no avail. One day, catastrophe struck! Her husband of ten years mysteriously died. As if that was not enough, she lost her brother in law and father in law too. You can imagine the amount of pain she had to go through. Every lady has fine dreams of how lovely her home would look like. All those dreams had collapsed in a single day like a pack of cards.

But somewhere along the line, she had come to know the God of Israel, the God of Naomi. They had shared deep sorrow, great affection for each other and now an overriding commitment to the God of Israel. One day, Naomi decided to go back to her homeland, leaving Ruth with the option of the remaining in Moab.

Lessons from her life include:

- She did not choose the easy way out

- She was sincere in her heart
- She was not lazy
- She was willing and obedient

1. *Our first lesson is that Ruth did not choose the easy way out.* She was committed to the cause she believed in, even at the expense of her life.

Not knowing what was in store for her in Judah, she still stuck to her commitment to God and Naomi even when given an opportunity to compromise.

Ruth 1:16, "But Ruth replied, "Don't urge me to leave you or to turn back from you. Where you go I will go and where you stay I will stay. Your people will be my people and your God my God".

Oh! How great her commitment was. Many believers today, when presented with an opportunity to compromise, will usually take the easiest way out saying "God understands". How many can say like Ruth, I will not turn back. She was not following Naomi per se but actually the God of Naomi, through Naomi because she was her only point of contract and reference.

There is always a pathway of least resistance, it is always easier to go with the crowd, but Ruth led an exemplary life of deep conviction and persuasion in what she believed in.

2. *Our second lesson is sincerity of heart.*

Ruth was sincere and loyal. She enjoyed a relationship that involved mutual respect and commitments with Naomi. Oh how I wish that such relationships would abound in the body of Christ today? That we would stop envying and stabbing each other's backs and operates in total sincerity of heart. A battle axe cannot afford to keep malice or be a spreader of rumors and mischief. If you are doing such, please desist today! Let us indeed be bonded together with the sacrificial love of Christ, bearing each other's burdens. Speak sincerely, relate sincerely with all purity and simplicity of heart. Matthew 18:3, *"And he said, I tell you the truth, unless you change and become like little children, you will never enter the kingdom of heaven"*. Children are sincere hearts. Jesus therefore urged his disciples to be child like (not childish) in nature. This is very important because a lot of revival fire have died because the body of Christ has refused to work together as one. Yet, the fire of revival cannot be rekindled in the midst of envy, jealousy and dissentions. We must learn to work together. We may not be the same but we are one.

May God help us to possess a sincere and simple heart. Amen!

3. *Our third lesson is that Ruth was not lazy., she took the initiative.*

Many Christians have turned Jesus into a magician and not a miracle worker. We do not want to make any input yet we expect to reap bountiful harvest. Rather than work with our hands, we prefer to spend our days away in the name of praying. We erroneously forget that faith without works is useless. James 2:17, *"In the same way, faith by itself, if it is not accompanied by action, is dead"*.

We see Ruth in Ruth 2:2, *"And Ruth the Moabitess said to Naomi, "Let me go to the fields and pick up the leftover grain behind anyone in whose eyes I find favor"*. She was a widow and according to the Israelite law, could have depended on the government to feed her but she chose to move out of her comfort zone and provide for her needs. She went to work. She was not afraid of admitting her needs or working hard to supply it. If you are waiting for God to provide, consider this: He may be waiting for you to take the first step to demonstrate just how important your need is.

Though she did not have a farm of her own, she made the best out of the situation she found herself by picking up grains that were leftover from other people's farm as was customary. Yet, some people are so lazy that despite the fact that they do not have their own farm, they would still not be able to go out and pick. Probably they expect manna to drop physically from heaven. Brethren, Christianity is not an excuse for laziness. Rather, it must be the driving force for diligence and excellence.

Ruth's task, though menial, tiring and perhaps degrading, was done faithfully. What is your attitude when the task you have been giving is not up to your potential/ the task at hand may be all you can do or it may be the work God wants you to do or as in Ruth's case, attest of your character that may open new doors of opportunity for you. What is your attitude to the task at hand?

4. *Our fourth lesson is that she was willing and obedient.*
Right from the time of Noah, God had promised that His Spirit will not strive with man any longer. The Holy Spirit speaks to us in a still small voice, convincing and prodding us gently in the right way. Yet many of us turn deaf ears. We stubbornly decide to go our own way, thinking we are wise in our eyes. Forgetting that God sees the end from the beginning. Beloved, Ruth had Naomi as a Godly counselor but beautifully now, you have the Holy Spirit as your first counselor, do you yield to him? Please, would you make up your mind to say like Ruth said: *"I will do whatever you say"* (Ruth 3:5).

In conclusion, Ruth's life exhibited admirable qualities: she was loving, brave, hardworking, kind and faithful. These gained her a good reputation but only because she displayed them consistently in all areas of her life. A good reputation comes by consistently living out your belief system which must be formed on the basis of the Word. Thus, she strategically positioned herself as a battle axe in the lineage of grace to herald the coming of the Messiah.

Just as Ruth was unaware of the purpose of God for her life, we may not fully understand God's dealings over our lives until we look retrospectively from the side of eternity. But we must make our choices with God's eternal values in mind. Taking moral short cuts and living or short range pleasures will take us nowhere. Live in faithfulness to God, knowing that the significance of your life will extend beyond your lifetime.

Chapter Four

HOW TO SUSTAIN OUR EFFECTIVENESS

4 HOW TO SUSTAIN OUR EFFECTIVENESS

Taking a look at the disciples of Jesus , they were not extra ordinary people. They were singled out to be co-labourers in the initial apostolic wave, just as God is in business of selecting men to join the end time army. They were people ready to leave everything to do the master's bidding.

Examples abound in the Bible of such men and women that were nothing according to human standards but were chosen by God to do exploits. And so I discovered that God's greatest desire is to draw mankind into his manifold love and kindness, to make use of us as a shining light in this present world of thick darkness, so that ultimately, only His name would be glorifies. The big question now is this: what are the requirements of the master?{ what are the qualities that a man must have in his CV in order to be enrolled for the master's use ? How do I sustain my effectiveness?

Before discussing any point, I must at this juncture, mention that every battle axe willingly submit himself/herself to be recruited into this end time army. God has never forced man to make any decisions. God created man with the ability to choose. So you must be available to God.

Isaiah 6-8,
"Then I heard the voice of the Lord saying, "Whom shall I send? And who will go for us" And I said, "HERE AM I. SEND ME!"

You must first heed the call of salvation and then the call of service. The call to pick up your cross and follow Him daily. That wherever he leads you will go. And whatever He says you will do. Beloved, are you really available to God? Can God get your attention amidst your busy schedule? Have you not planned your life, your ambition and goals that there is no space for God? Will you let go of your life and hand it over to God to be used for His glory?

Furthermore, the following virtues are essential victuals we must carry with us.

- Purity
- Brokenness
- Diligence
- Sensitivity/discernment

1. *PURITY*

The hallmark of a life that will be useful for God is purity. The Psalmist asked a question Psalm 24, that who will be able to ascend the holy hill of God and stand in his very presence? The answer is simple: he who has clean hands and a pure heart. The basic quality that God requires from us is to keep ourselves pure. Permit me to dwell a bit on this matter, purity, because it is a topic that has long been forgotten. It is hardly preached anymore on our altars because it has been overtaken more interesting topics such as "Prosperity", "Ten ways to get your right husband/wife in ten days", "The seven shortcuts to becoming rich", "Ten weapon to kill all your enemies" etc. please do not get wrong, it is not that all these aspects of our live are not important but we should not also leave the weightier matter unaddressed.

2Timothy 2:19-22; "But God's truth stands firm like a foundation stone with the inscription: "The Lord knows those who are his, " and all who belong to the Lord must turn away from evil. In a wealthy home, some utensils are made of gold and silver, and some are made of wood and clay.
The expensive utensils are used for special occasions and he cheap ones are for everyday use. IF YOU KEEP YOURSELF PURE, YOU WILL BE A SPECIAL UTENSIL FOR HONOURABLE USE. YOUR LIFE WILL BE CLEAN AND YOU WILL BE READY FOR THE

MASTER TO USE YOU FOR EVERY GOOD WORK. Run from anything that stimulates youthful lusts. Instead pursue righteous living, faithfulness, love and peace. Enjoy the companionship of those who call on the Lord with pure hearts. (NLT)

Unfortunately, purity and holiness are not reflected in how long the skirt of a sister is or in how well you can speak in tongues. No! these are not the yardsticks. Purity and holiness refer to the state of a man's heart. It refers to the total purging and consecration of one's heart from all forms of contamination, dross and impediments. It is the circumcision of our hearts (a circumcision not made of physical hands0 such that we will able to present ourselves as a living sacrifice, holy and acceptable to God. One of the Bible class students asked me, if it is possible to live a holy life? My answer was yes! It is very possible. If it was not so, Jesus would not have said that, 1Peter 1:15-16 *"But just as He who called you is holy, so be holy in all you do. For it is written, "Be holy, because I am holy".* Also the scriptures tell us in Hebrew 12:24, *"Make every effort to live in peace with all men and to be holy; without holiness no one will see the Lord".* Please do not be deceived by the recent wave of carnality carrying people around these days, saying that it is not possible to be holy. I stand to emphatically state based on the scriptures that a lifestyle of utmost holiness and discipline is attainable and it is in fact, God's standard.

God is not a respecter of persons. He will not reduce His standards because of anybody. Therefore, we must take heed and ensure that we play the game according to His own rules. Our God is a holy God, so kindly decide today to purge your life of any form of contamination. Stand in His righteousness and walk in purity.

2. BROKENNESS

Another ingredient of a life that will be useful to God is Brokenness. That is humility, a gentle spirit. Proverbs 6:16-17. *"There are six things the Lord hates, seven that are detestable to him: haughty eyes, a lying tongue, hands that shed innocent blood"*. The psalmist said that a humble and contrite heart the Lord will not reject. The woman with the alabaster box of oil that anointed the feet of Jesus when He went to dine in the house of Simon had to break open the box before the oil could be released to serve the purpose that God wanted it to serve. So also, we have these riches of treasures in an earthen vessel that must be brought under subjection to the Holy Spirit. Only brokenness will allow God to achieve what He wants to do in our lives. God does not have anything to do with a proud man. Pride is the state of a man's heart and not the outcome appearance of seemingly looking gentle.

Many take pride in flaunting their weaknesses, they tell

you "that is the way I am and that's all" but it should not be so. Every day, we must be willing to let God work on our lives, chiseling away chips and bits of us, till we attain the level of perfection He desires in us.

3. DILIGENCE

A lot of believers are complacent. We have become complacent about our prayer life, our study life or the intensity with which we evangelize. A lot of our exploits re testimonies of five or ten years ago, we seem to relish the victories of the past rather than forgetting the past and pressing on. Some have erroneously believed that because salvation is not based on good deeds, they could live their lives any way they wanted. If you truly belong to God , like Peter wrote in 2 Peter 1:10, your hard work will prove it. We must make our calling and election sure by our readiness to discipline ourselves, get out of our comfort zones and be a battle axe for God.

Some, on the other hand, have become discouraged. To stand alone could be difficult at times. Everybody else doing the wrong thing seems to be getting away with it. Sometimes, we may find ourselves envying how the wicked prosper. This may cause us to lose our vigor and fervency. Please, be encouraged. Hear what God says,

Hebrews 6:10-12, *"God is not unjust; he will not forget your work and the love you have shown him as you have helped his people and continue to help them. We want each of you to show this same diligence to the very end, I order to make your hope sure. We do not want you to become lazy but to imitate those who through faith and patience inherit what has been promised".*

Let God's love for you and his intimate knowledge of your service for Him bolster you as face disappointment and rejection here on earth. Hope keeps thee Christian from becoming lazy or feeling bored. Each time I imagine the face of the Master on that judgment day as he welcomes me home, I feel rejuvenated that the reward lies ahead. Like a soldier, a battle axe for the Lord, press on!

4. *SHARPNESS/SENSITIVITY/DISCERNMENT*

As Christians, we are soldiers for Christ. We are to be fully armed, never relenting, watching and praying till all our foes are vanquished. Please note, we are not fighting against any man. Our fight is not against the witch in your village or the boss that has refused to grant you promotion or that friend of yours that has betrayed your trust . No! We are not wrestling against flesh and blood. 2Corinthians 10:3, *"For though we live in the world, we do not wage war as the world does".* And so because our target is not flesh and blood, we cannot make use of physical weapons either. Our armor is a spiritual armor, made of spiritual weapons sharpened in the place of spiritual warfare.

Some Christians unfortunately and erroneously believe that there is nothing as spiritual warfare. I used to have a friend that believed that demons do not exist. Beloved, demons do exist, Matthew 8:31, 9:33, 17:18; Luke 9:42. The following scriptures bear account of people who were demon possessed in the Bible: Matthew 4:24, 9:16,8:28, 9:32,2:22; Mark 1:32, 5:16; Luke 8:27, 8:36; John 7:20, 8:48, 10:20; Acts 19:13. The spiritual world is real. We may not see demons walking about in the market in broad daylight but their activities are real around us. People who have had spiritual attacks and encounters will understand this better. I have had spiritual confrontations, learnt to engage in spiritual warfare at a very young age and so I know beyond doubt that the spiritual world is real. During the course of ministering deliverance for people, I have seen demons speak through people, twisting and turning them as they left. So I know that the spiritual world is real. The same way we know that God exists though we have not seen Him face to face.

Ephesians 6:12, *'For our struggle is not against flesh and blood but against the rulers, against the authorities, against the powers of this dark world and against the spiritual forces of evil in the heavenly realms'*.

Therefore, we must be very sensitive to the leading of the Holy Spirit. A lot of believers, painfully, have become casualties on the battle field because of carelessness. Remember , the devil always roams around, waiting for our unguarded moments to hunt us down. We should not take anything for granted, make no assumptions.

I'VE ENLISTED IN THE ARMY
OF THE LORD TODAY

I've enlisted in the army of the Lord today,
Fighting ever for the truth and right;
Safely guided by Jehovah in the king's highway,
He will lead his army day and night.

I've enlisted in the army of the heavenly king,
Tho' the battle may be fierce and long;
Someday, I shall come rejoicing and my trophies bring,
Then I'll sing and about shout the victor' song.

A.R. Walton

WILL YOU BE A BATTLEAXE FOR GOD?

5 WILL YOU BE A BATTLE AXE FOR GOD?

We have reached a critical point after all has been said, you must make a decision. Will you be a battle axe for God? Will you be a voice for him in the wilderness pointing to the world the way to go by walking there yourself? Will you be a useful vessel in the hand of the master to do as he wishes with you?

Do you think you have disappointed God? Beloved, it is not too late. No matter how far away you have turned, you can return today to the shepherd of your soul in repentance and He will gladly accept you. No matter how red your slate of sin may be, He can make it spotless. That is what grace is all about. JUST COME!

Peradventure, there is a call of God over your life and you know it. So strongly, so surely. Yet, you have found it difficult to respond to. You have given excuses over and over again. Will you repent today and heed the call of God over your life? Leave everything and follow in total obedience. Yield the Master's call that you are ready, ready to serve even at the cost of your life.

Make this declaration:

"I am a seed, destined for a divine purpose ultimately. The seed may pass through storms of life in reaching that result but my end I will reach, my purpose I will fulfill. I may sometimes frustrate the grace of God over my life but I will not frustrate His will. I may be disappointed at times in failing to be what I would like to be and what I imagine I might have been but I will not give up. I will press on until I become the best God created me to be.

I willingly submit my life, my dreams, ambitions, prestige and honor at the feet of the cross. Choosing rather to go the way of self-denial and service. The world behind me, I press on! No turning back.

I choose to be a battle axe, available, sharp, strong and prepared for the master's use. I will be diligent. Enable me through your divine grace to live a pure life and deal with others with a sincere heart.

I choose to stand for Christ, even if it means standing alone.

SO HELP ME GOD!

"Your place is kept and it will wait
Ready for you to fill, soon or late:
Better soon because another may be appointed

To fill your place in the army,
No star is ever lost,
Will heaven continue to wait for you?"

CONCLUSION

CONCLUSION

God created us to be extensions of His life here on earth. He redeemed us with His blood and gave us power to establish His kingdom here on earth. Therefore, God needs you. He needs us to do His will, to meet His need. There is always a search in Heaven, searching for who will be a useful, available weapon in the hands of the master.

Amazingly however, He is not moved by the outward displays we put up. The Lord is rather, in the business of taking ordinary people to accomplish His purposes. Nobody is useless. We are members of God's army and He is the commander.

In order to be an effective battle axe, we need to be completely grounded in the word and continually filled with the Holy Spirit. We all have a responsibility in the Lord's army and for us to be influence we need to yield and allow God to direct our ways, we are the axe in His hands, just as clay in the hands of the potter.

It is my sincere desire that your eyes of understanding be opened and your hearts enlightened as you heed the call to meet the need of the master at a time like this.

Shalom!

Till we meet at the Master's feet,
Remain Rapturable.